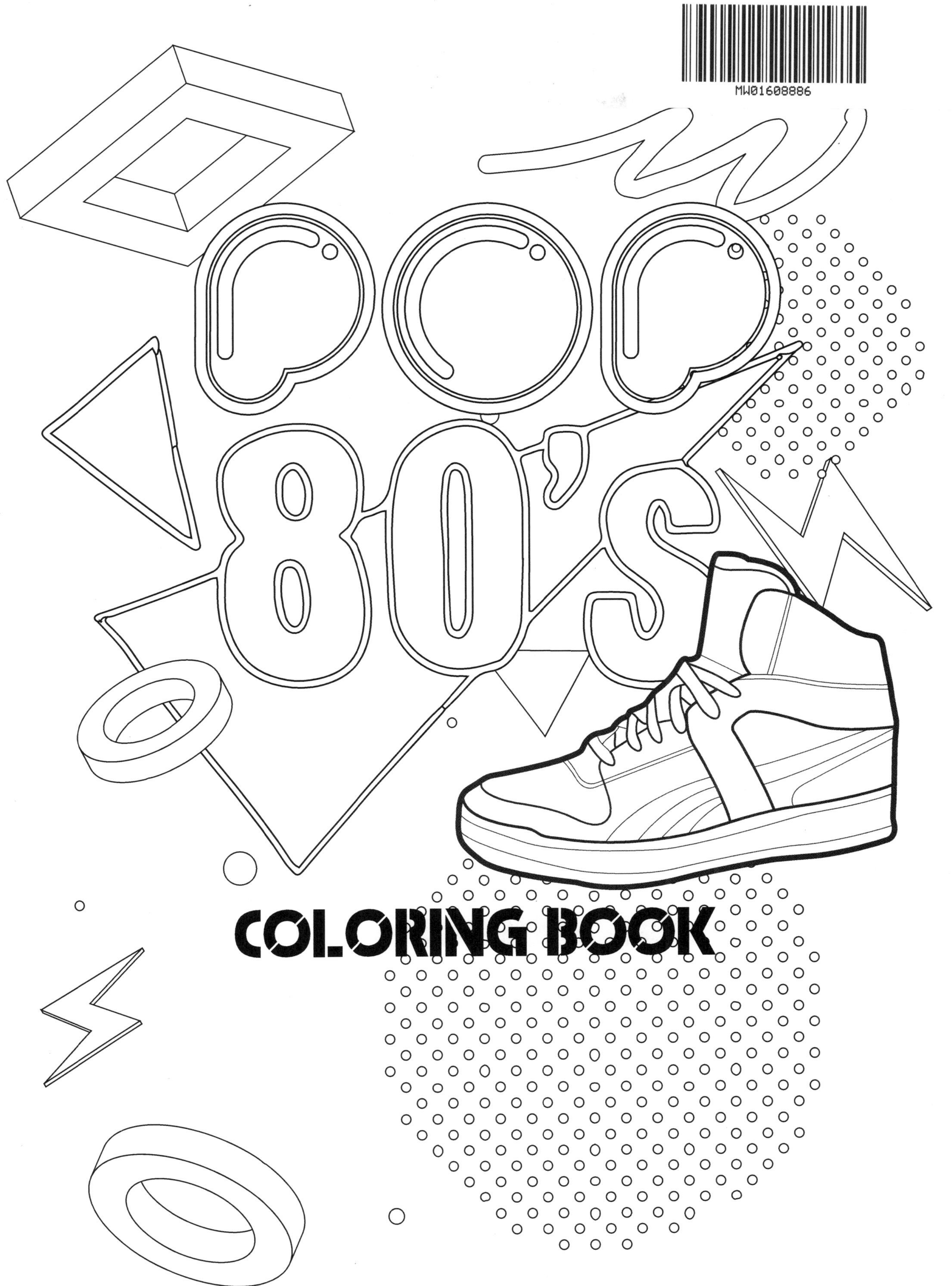

POP 80's
COLORING BOOK
MW01608886

illustrated by
DAVID GIRALDO
juandamurai

INDEX
A *DATE/TIME *NOISE REDUCTION
B *DATE/TIME *NOISE REDUCTION
1. SITCOM
2. ACTION SERIES
3. ANIMES
4. MOVIES
5. TV LATINO

SIT COM
ALF
ALF (or Alien Life Form) is a creature from Planet Melmac that crash landed on earth, and is adopted/taken in by an otherwise normal Earth family. A comedic sitcom that featured episodes with everything from mundane things like getting people to like you, to close calls with the government, all with the added spice of Alf making life more difficult and interesting for all involved. The wise cracking alien, with a taste for cats (and we don't mean as pets) spent many years as a beloved TV icon for a good reason.

ALF

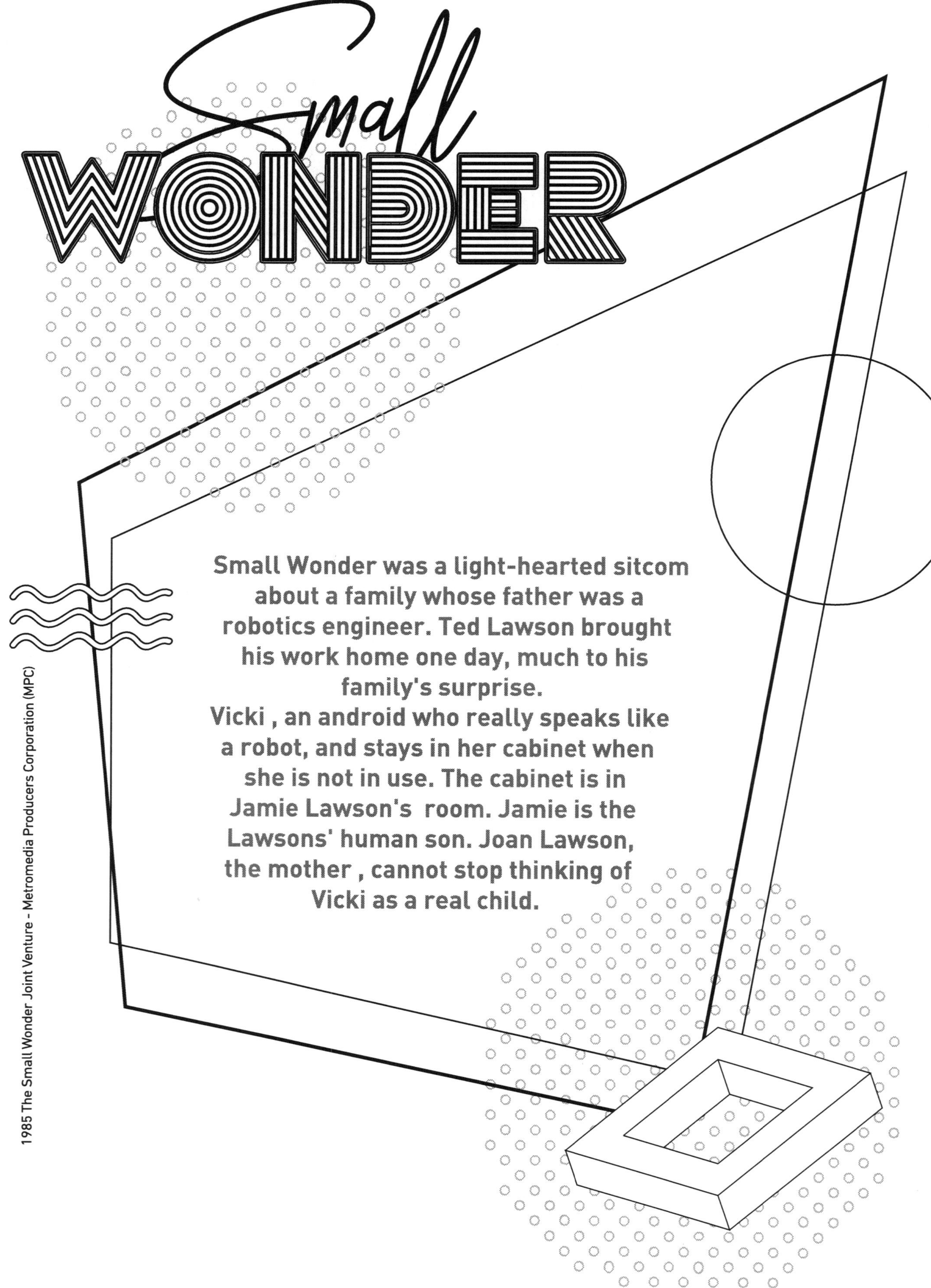

Small
WONDER

Small Wonder was a light-hearted sitcom about a family whose father was a robotics engineer. Ted Lawson brought his work home one day, much to his family's surprise.
Vicki , an android who really speaks like a robot, and stays in her cabinet when she is not in use. The cabinet is in Jamie Lawson's room. Jamie is the Lawsons' human son. Joan Lawson, the mother , cannot stop thinking of Vicki as a real child.

1985 The Small Wonder Joint Venture – Metromedia Producers Corporation (MPC)

Vicky

The Greatest American Hero
1981 Stephen J. Cannell Productions – Created By Stephen J. Cannell

ACTION SERIFS

When aliens come to Earth to ask for our help, a few suspicious humans discover their horrific true intentions and prepare to resist. Aliens pretending to be friendly come to Earth and are received openly. The aliens have masqueraded themselves to look just like humans. When it is discovered that the aliens' planet is dying and that they have come to rape the Earth of its natural resources, the war for Earth begins. An important key to the humans' success is distinguishing the their own from the aliens.

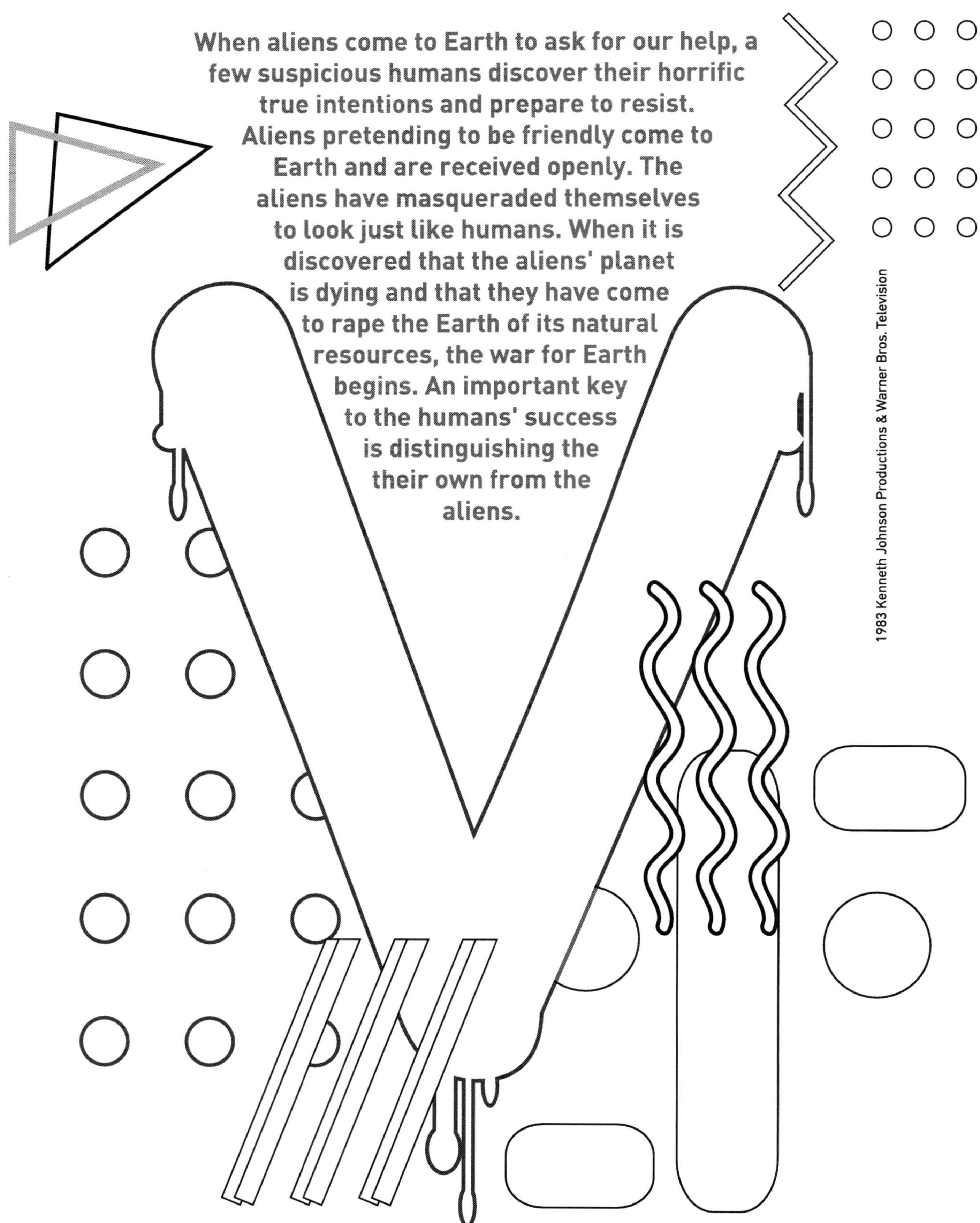

Diana

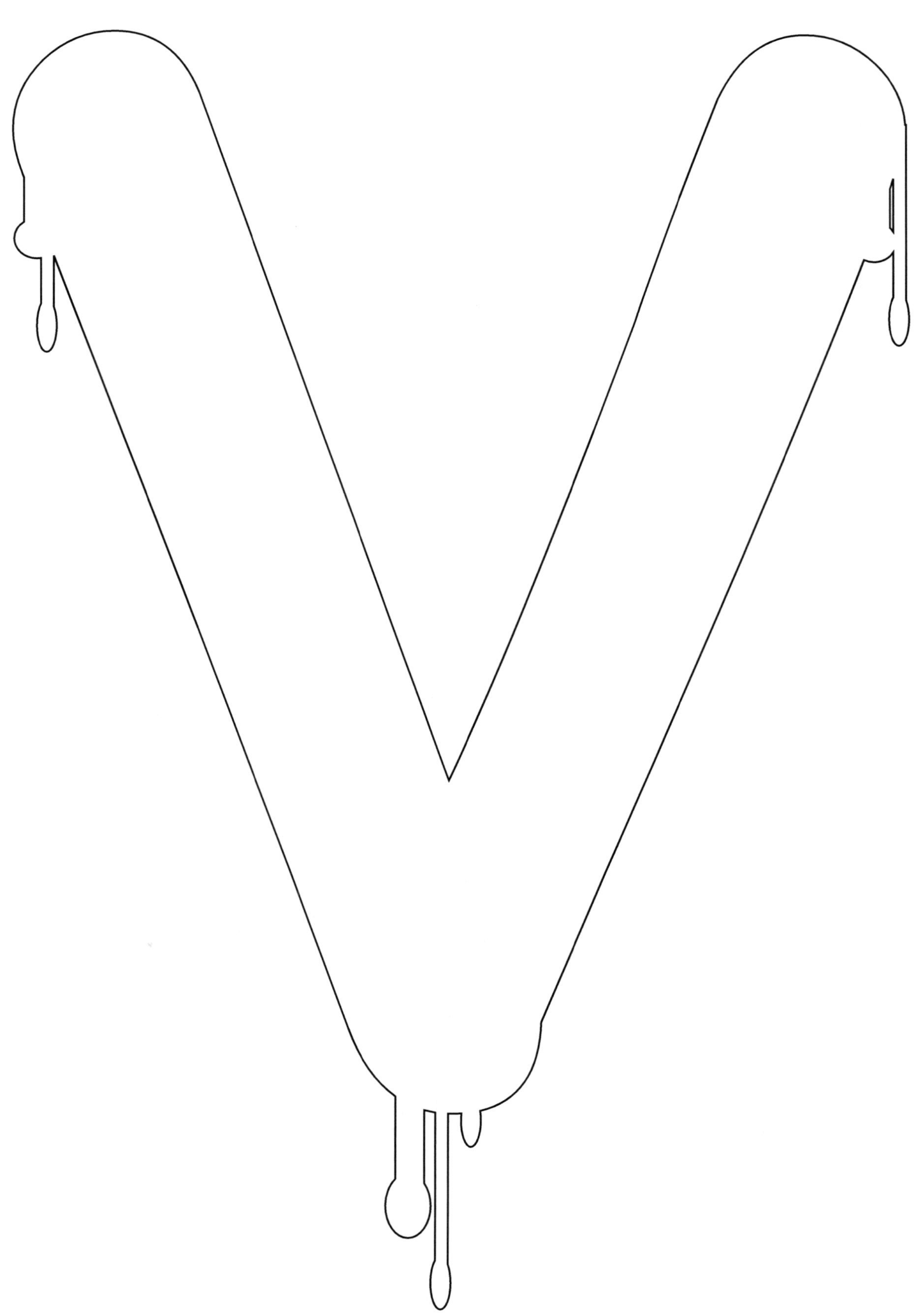

Donovan

THE

A

TEAM.

In 1972, a crack commando unit was sent to prison by a military court for a crime they didn't commit. These men promptly escaped from a maximum-security stockade to the Los Angeles underground. Today, still wanted by the government, they survive as soldiers of fortune. If you have a problem, if no one else can help, and if you can find them, maybe you can hire The A-Team.

Anibal Smith

Fas

B ☆ A
Baracus

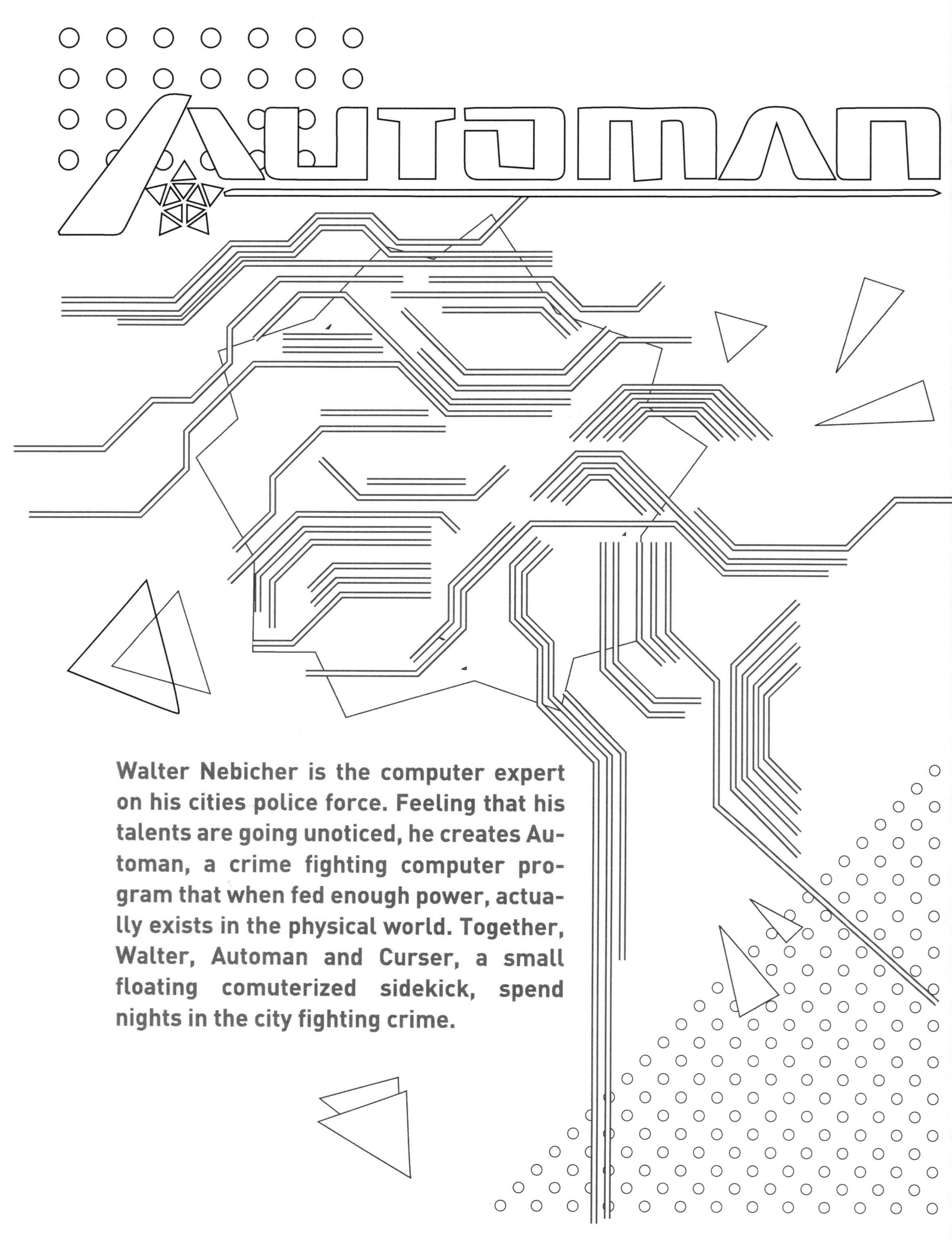

Walter Nebicher is the computer expert on his cities police force. Feeling that his talents are going unoticed, he creates Automan, a crime fighting computer program that when fed enough power, actually exists in the physical world. Together, Walter, Automan and Curser, a small floating comuterized sidekick, spend nights in the city fighting crime.

Automan

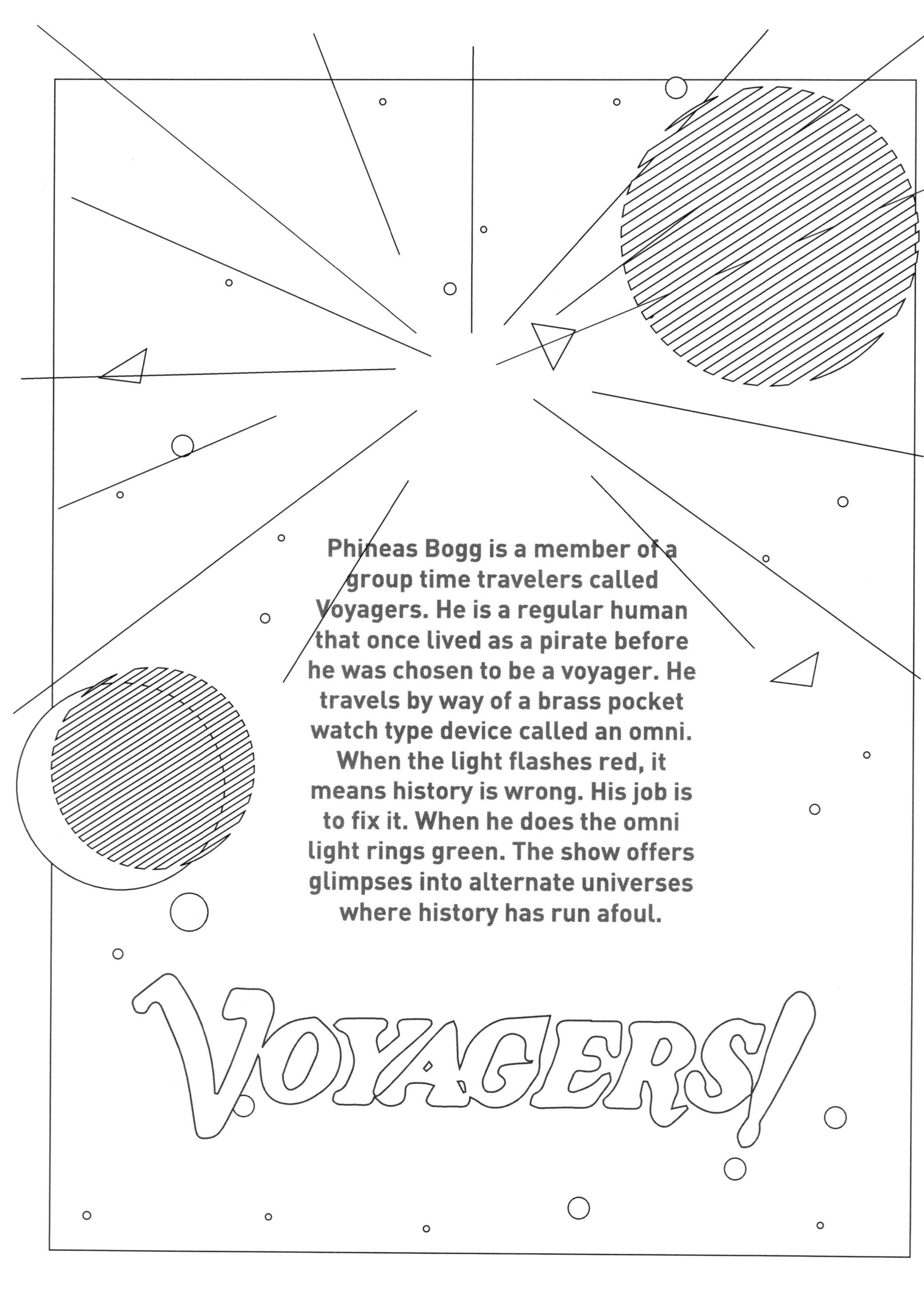

Phineas Bogg is a member of a group time travelers called Voyagers. He is a regular human that once lived as a pirate before he was chosen to be a voyager. He travels by way of a brass pocket watch type device called an omni. When the light flashes red, it means history is wrong. His job is to fix it. When he does the omni light rings green. The show offers glimpses into alternate universes where history has run afoul.

VOYAGERS!

SLEDGE
Action-packed thriller about a detective named Sledge Hammer and his beautiful, but not-so-bright partner Dori Doreau.
In each episode, Hammer and Doreau solve crimes and fight for justice.
HAMMER
TRUST ME -
I KNOW WHAT I'M DOING!

SLEGDE
Hammer

MANIMAL
Jonathan Chase is a British college professor at New York University who has the unusual ability to transform into any kind of animal he wants. He decides to use his power to assist the New York Police Department in solving unusual crimes, and in this series pilot, he teams up with cute cop Brooke and war buddy Ty to stop some terrorists from stealing a supply of toxic gas.

MANIMAL

QUANTUM
LEAP

Al Calavicci

Wonder Woman, based on Charles Moulton's comicbook superheroine of the 1940s, developed gradually into a regular TV series.
Wonder Woman

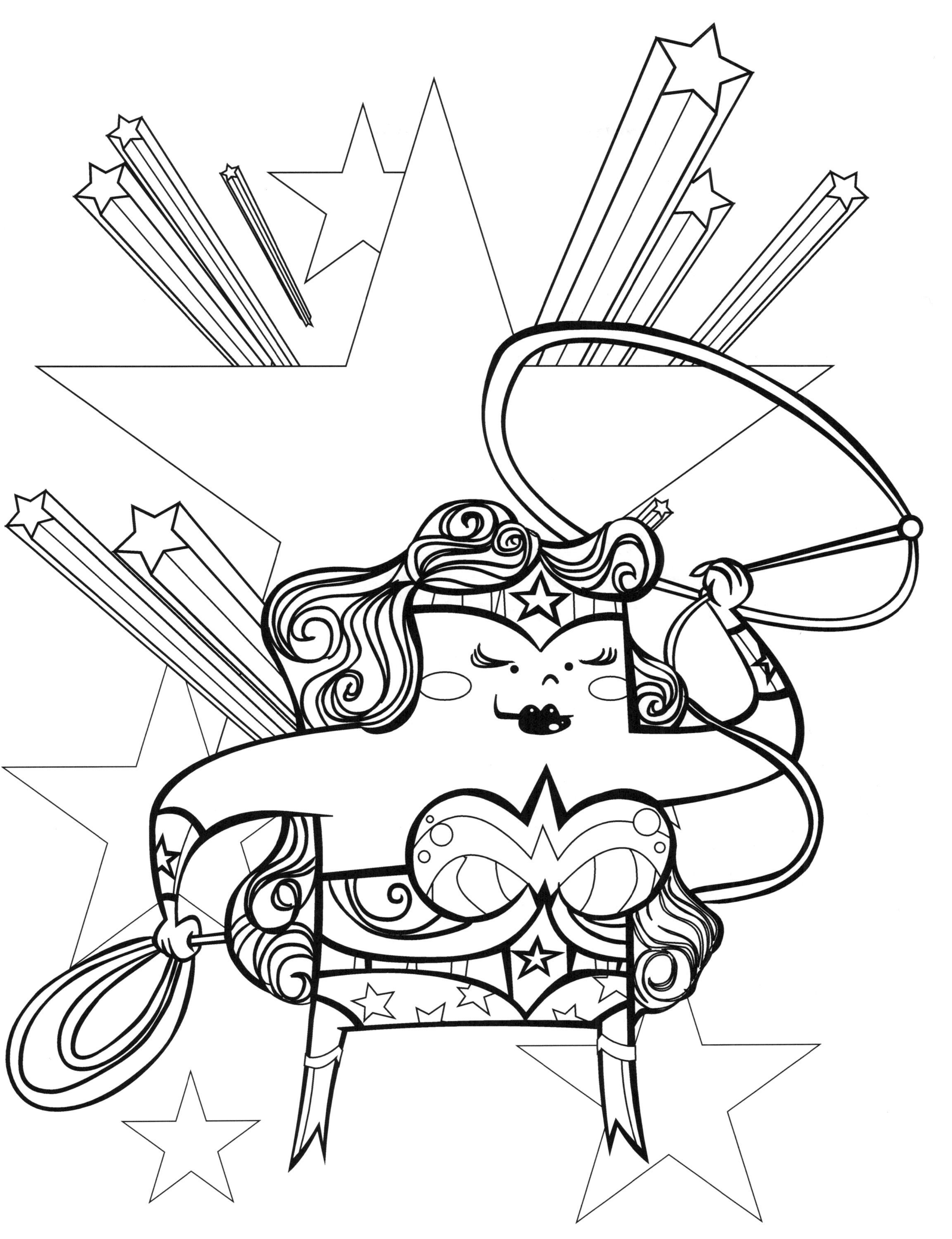

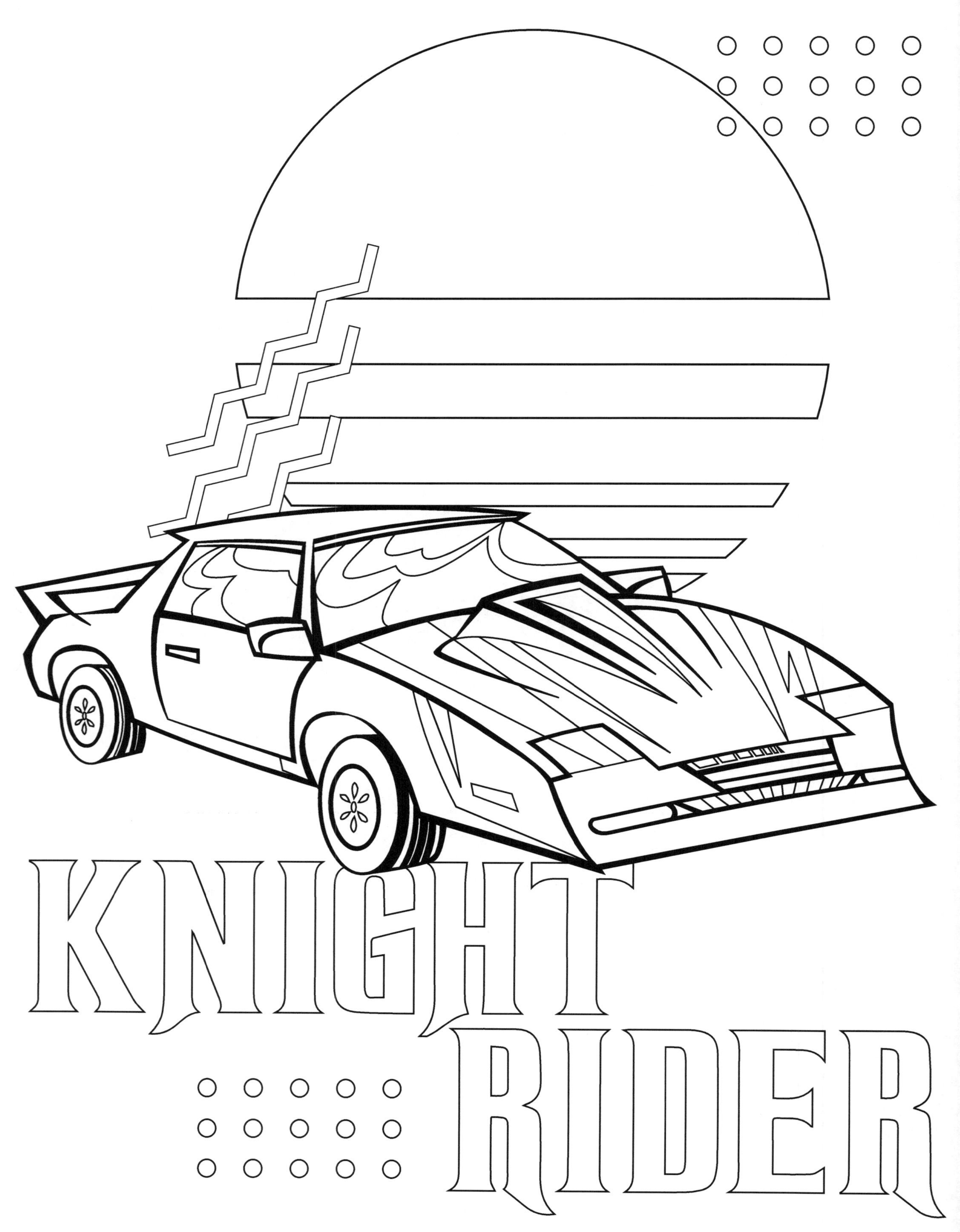

KNIGHT
RIDER

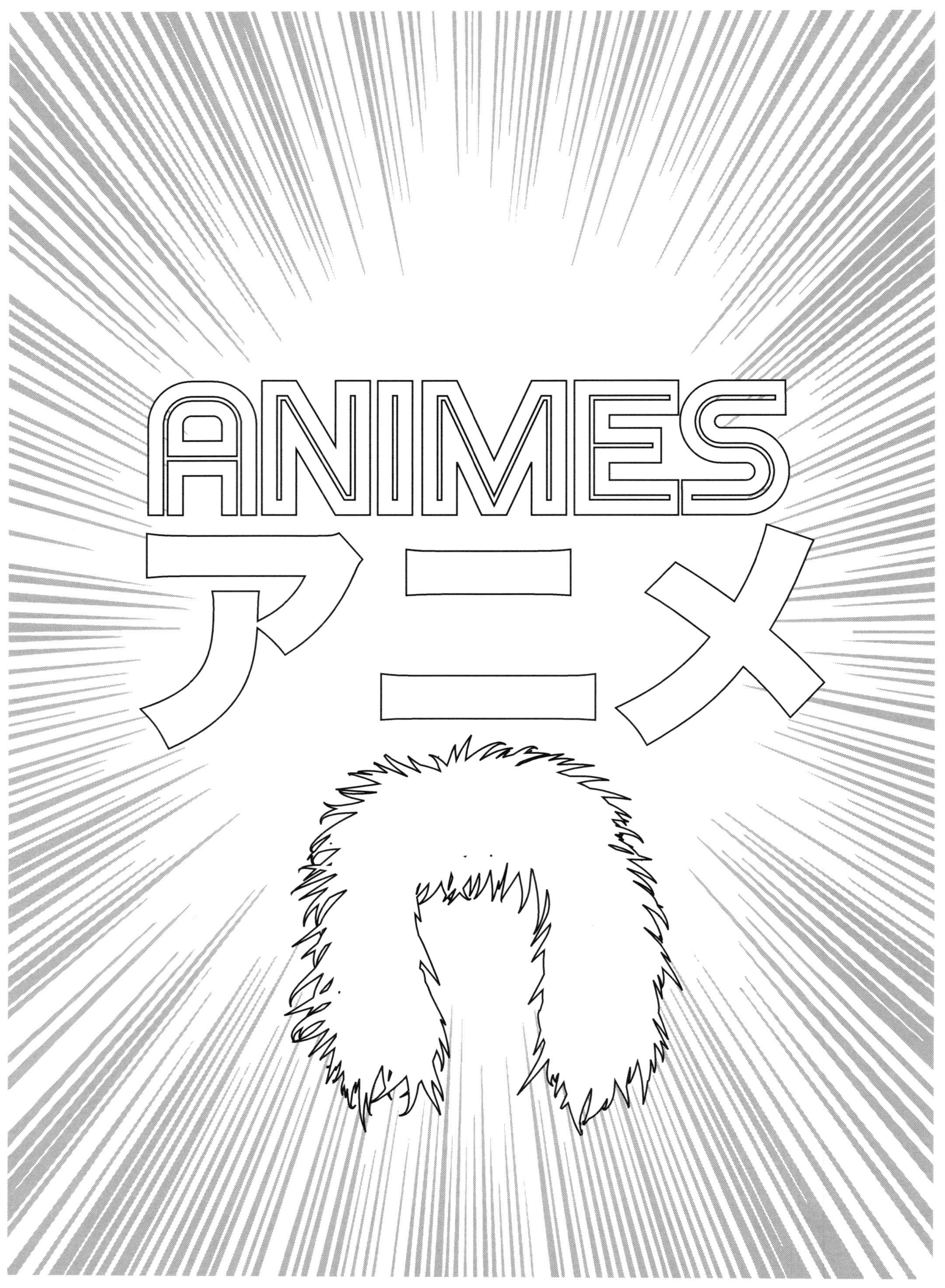

ANIMES
アニメ

GOKU

GENTELLA

月光仮面

moonlight mask

Moonlight Mask's identity has always been a mystery.

Decked out in white tights, a white & red cape, a white scarf, yellow gloves & boots, dark glasses, a cloth face mask and Indian-style turban (pinned with a "moon" ornament), Moonlight Mask is armed with a whip, two six-shooters, shuriken and moon-shaped boomerangs, and rides a motorcycle.

The show also became very popular in Latin America under the title Centella

CENTELLA

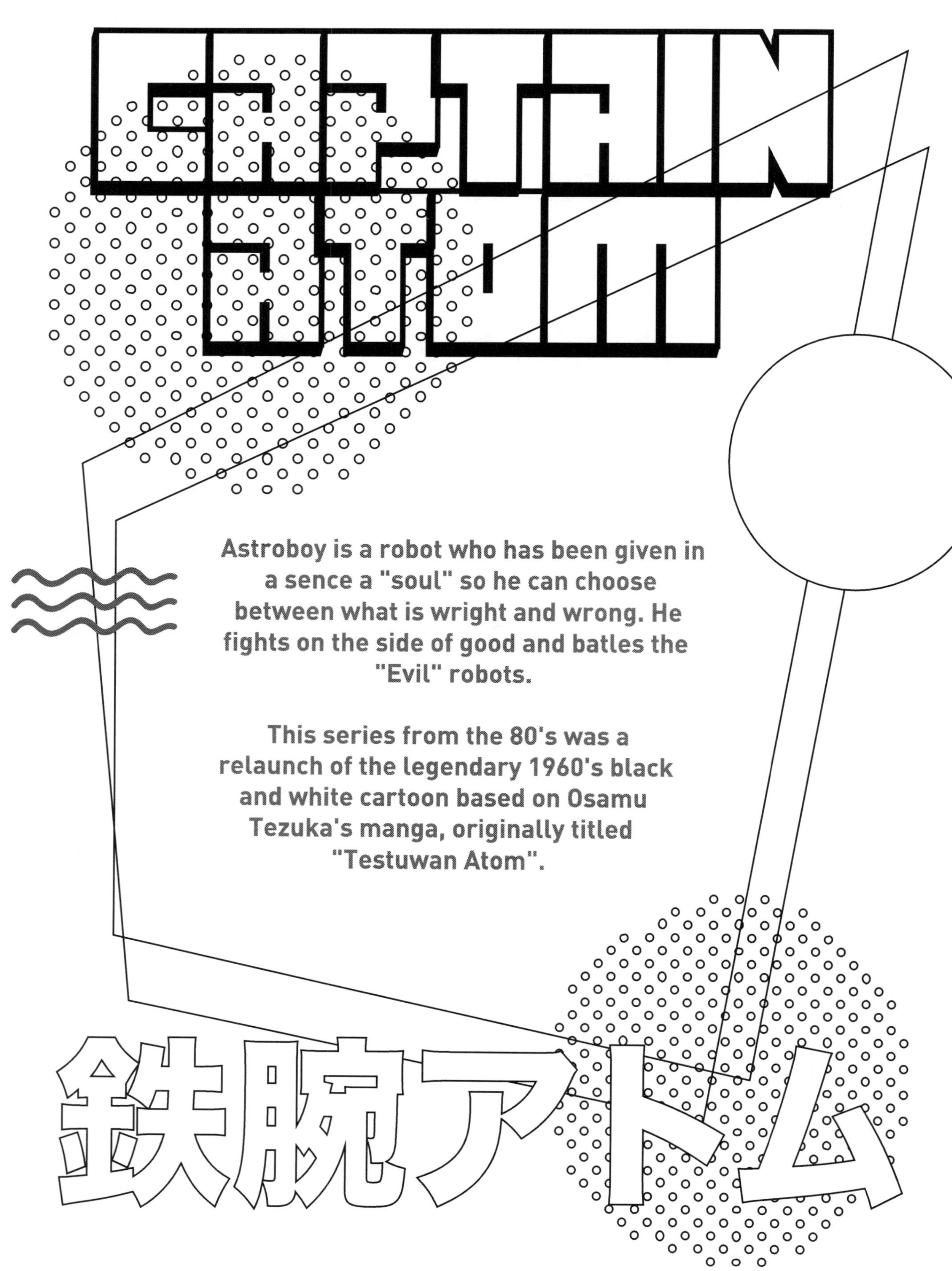

CAPTAIN ATOM

Astroboy is a robot who has been given in a sence a "soul" so he can choose between what is wright and wrong. He fights on the side of good and batles the "Evil" robots.

This series from the 80's was a relaunch of the legendary 1960's black and white cartoon based on Osamu Tezuka's manga, originally titled "Testuwan Atom".

鉄腕アトム

Astroboy

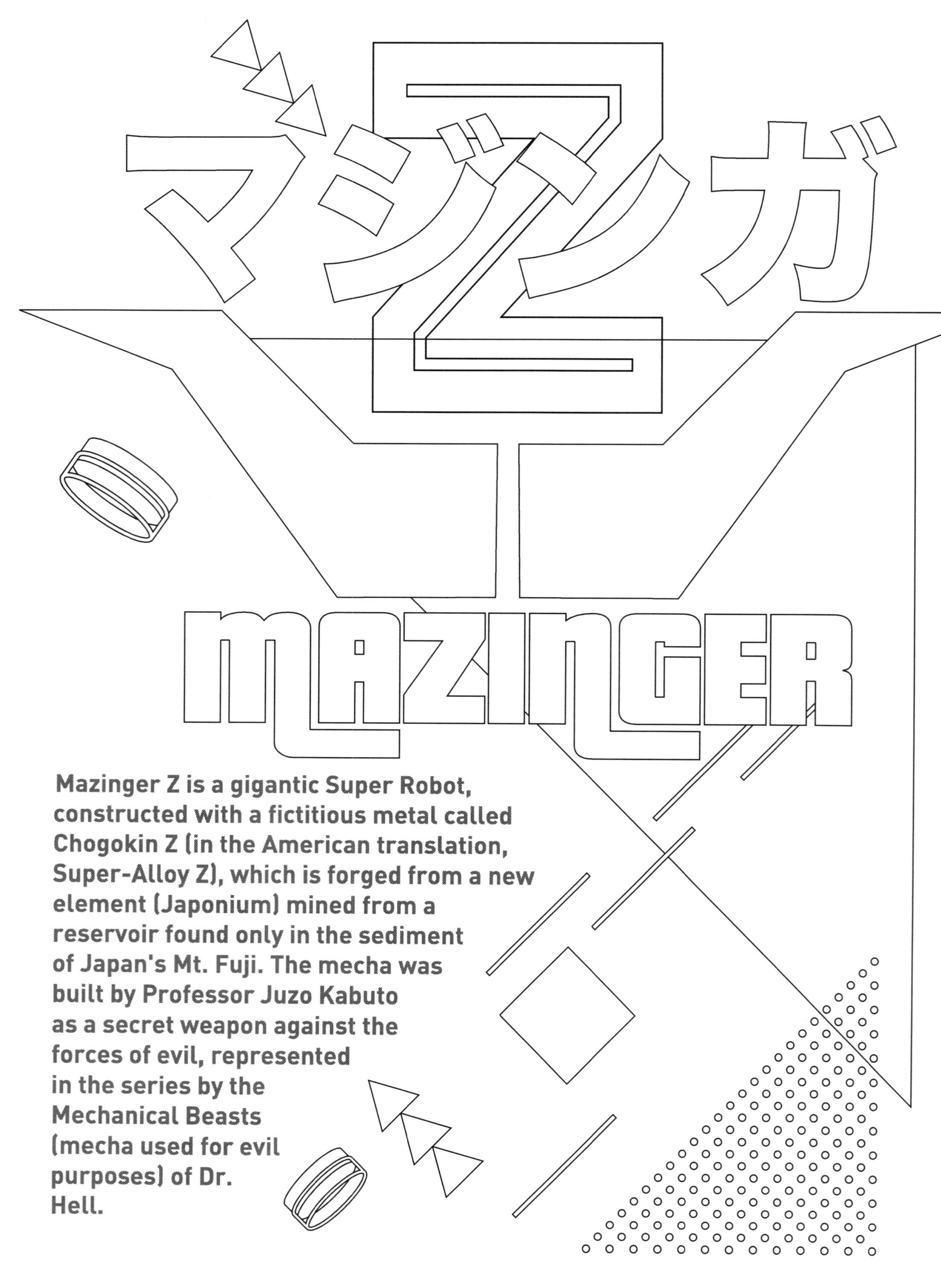

Mazinger Z is a gigantic Super Robot, constructed with a fictitious metal called Chogokin Z (in the American translation, Super-Alloy Z), which is forged from a new element (Japonium) mined from a reservoir found only in the sediment of Japan's Mt. Fuji. The mecha was built by Professor Juzo Kabuto as a secret weapon against the forces of evil, represented in the series by the Mechanical Beasts (mecha used for evil purposes) of Dr. Hell.

Mazinger

Afrodita

BOSS

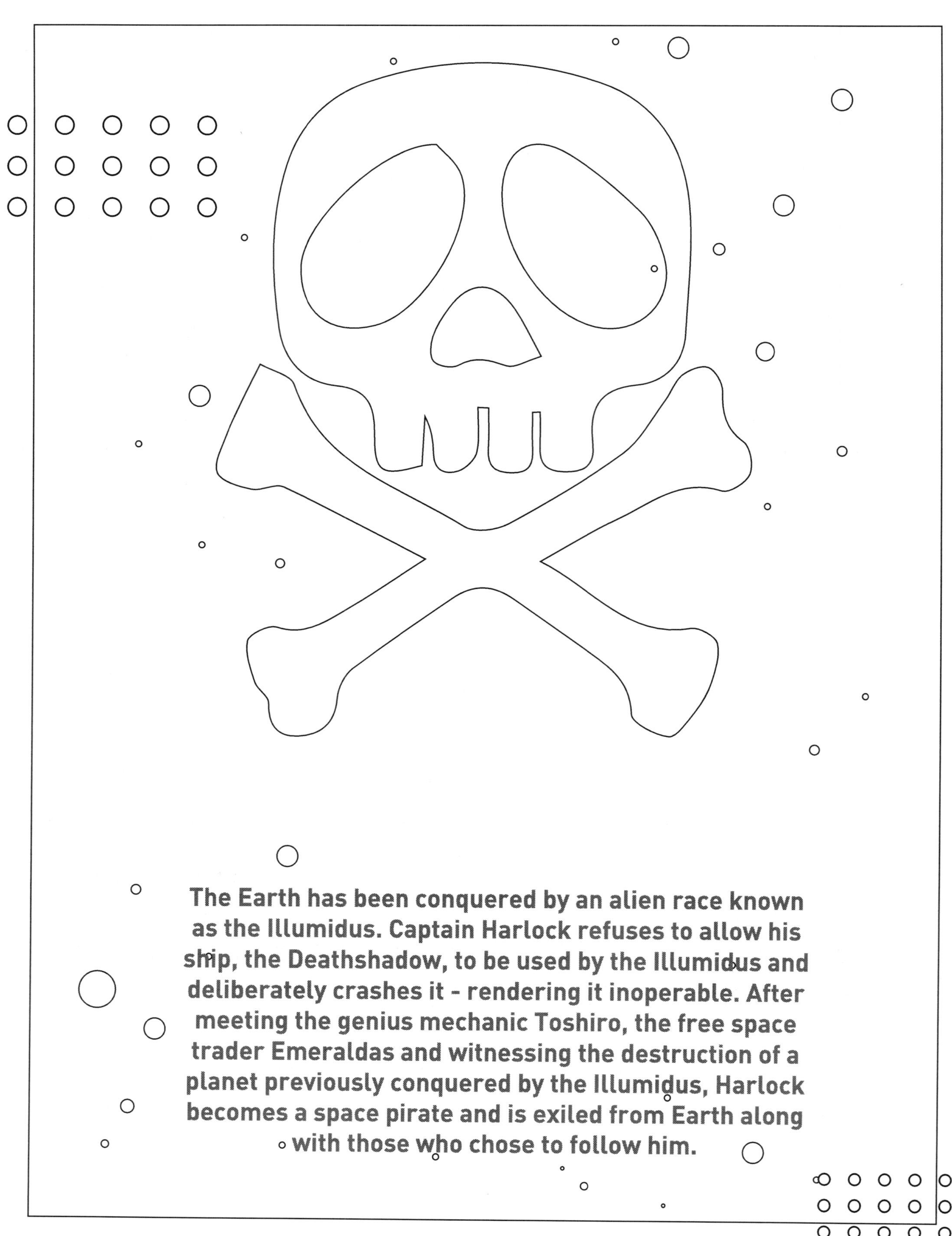

The Earth has been conquered by an alien race known as the Illumidus. Captain Harlock refuses to allow his ship, the Deathshadow, to be used by the Illumidus and deliberately crashes it - rendering it inoperable. After meeting the genius mechanic Toshiro, the free space trader Emeraldas and witnessing the destruction of a planet previously conquered by the Illumidus, Harlock becomes a space pirate and is exiled from Earth along with those who chose to follow him.

Harlock

DRAGON BALL Z
Doragon Bōru Zetto
ドラゴンボール

Dragon Ball
follows the adventures of the
protagonist Goku, a strong naïve boy
who, upon meeting Bulma, sets out to
gather the seven wish-granting Dragon
Balls. After becoming a student of martial
arts master Master Roshi, he and his fellow
pupil Krillin enter a tournament that attracts the
most powerful fighters in the world. He then
sets out on his own and winds up facing and des-
troying the Red Ribbon Army single-handedly.
When Krillin is later murdered after another
tournament, Goku exacts revenge on his
killer Piccolo Daimao. Three years
later, Goku, now a young adult,
must fight Piccolo Daimao's
offspring Piccolo.

GOKU

Vegeta

Emmanuelle

MOVIES
TICKET

INDIANA JONES

STAR WARS

BACK
TO THE FUTURE
5:29
Marty
McFly

Emeth Brown

Peter Venkman

RAY STANTZ
Ray
Stantz

ECTO-1
Egon
Spengler

TV
LATINO

He is an unemployed widower who lives with his daughter, Chilindrina, in the 72nd apartment in the Chavo neighborhood, owned by Mr. Barriga.

More agile than a turtle, stronger than a mouse,
nobler than a lettuce, his shield is a heart...
It's the Red Grasshopper!)

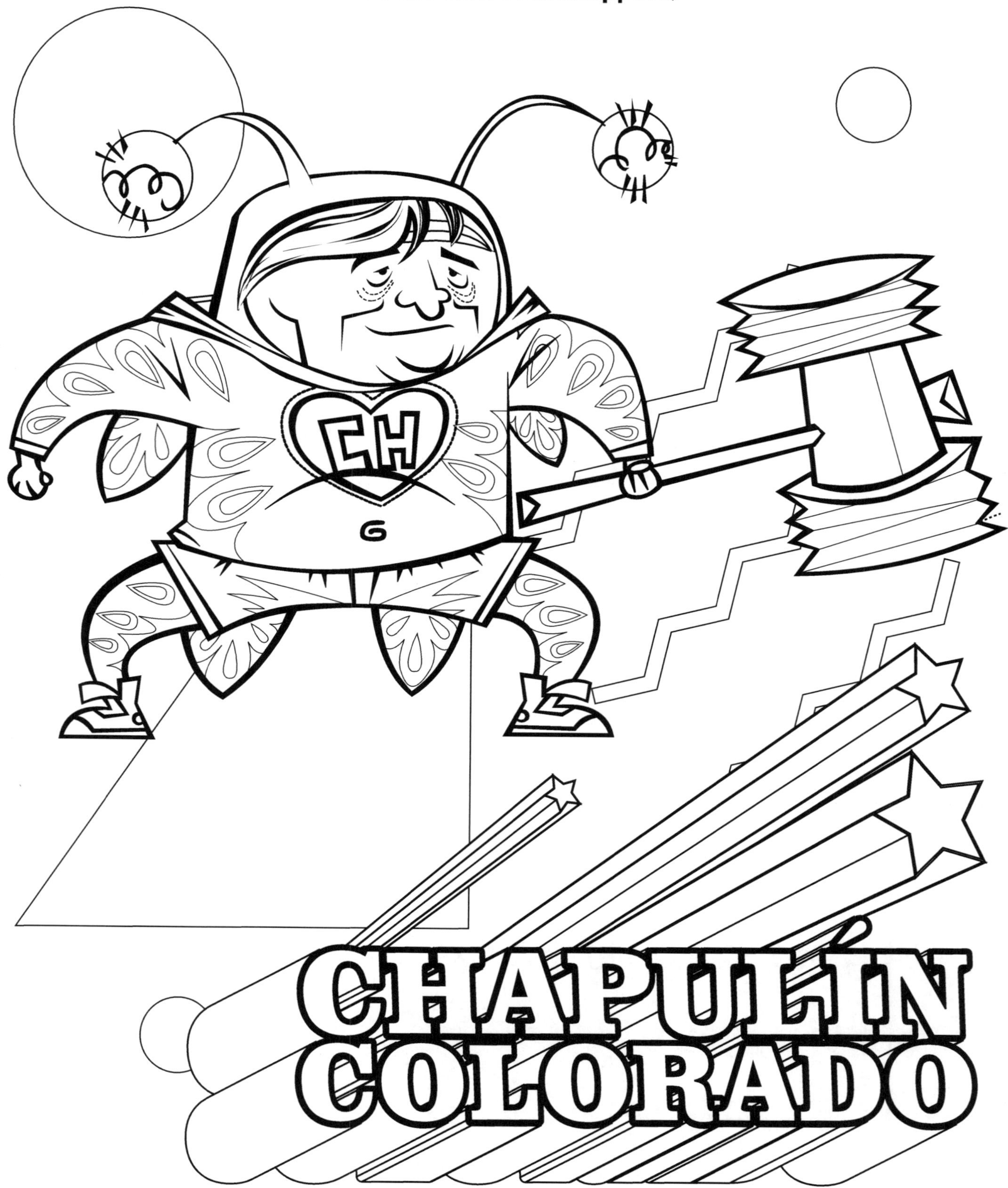

GURI-GURI

Guri Guri, the ally of Generoso the Guajiro, was a mecha-nical doll, it is the first Colombian telenovela where a doll is part of the cast.

The main character is Don Chinche (Francisco Eladio Chemas Mahecha), a mechanic, bricklayer and any other job he had to do to survive, along with his partner Eutimio Pastrana Polanía

つづく

Coming
soon

Coming
soon
DC
HEROES
COLORING BOOK